# Little Book Of Network Marketing Quotes

Thank you to all of the amazing people that I have come across in my journey thus far. You have all inspired me throughout my Network Marketing career.

I am constantly striving to learn more and improve myself in every aspect of life. Network Marketing is an incredible passion of mine that started out as a hobby and morphed into my purpose.

Through Network Marketing, you have the ability to not only transform your life, but to help others do the same. There is no greater joy in life than helping someone become financially free.

This book contains a list of 365+ Network Marketing quotes from all over the world to help motivate, inspire, and push you to become the best Network Marketing professional you can possibly be.

These quotes come from a wide range of top Network Marketing earners, authors, trainers, and motivational speakers. I have omitted all company names; this book is for our industry as a whole and not any one specific company.

Read one every morning to start your day off on the right foot in a positive mindset before the world has a chance to beat you down and play with your emotions.

The most powerful way to improve your Network Marketing business is to first change your way of thinking, and this book will help you with that. Read a quote every day, absorbing knowledge from the world's best Network Marketing professionals!

"An investment in knowledge pays the best interest."
—Benjamin Franklin

1. I would rather earn 1% of 100 people's efforts than 100% of my own.
   —J. Paul Getty

2. You are responsible "to" others, not "for" them; your responsibility is to show others and educate them on the opportunity.
   —Larry Raskin

3. In Network Marketing, it doesn't matter what works. It only matters what duplicates. —Eric Worre

4. If you help enough people get what they want, you will get what you want. —Zig Ziglar

5. It's crazy that some people feel that 2-5 years in a business is a long time to get rich, but don't feel that 40 years at a job is a long time to stay broke. —Unknown

6. You must as a leader have a plan, a step-by-step trail, and direct your people down the MLM power path. —Doug Firebaugh

7. Every great accomplishment is the sum of thousands of tiny accomplishments that no one sees or appreciates. —Brian Tracy

8. A goal is a dream with a deadline. —Napoleon Hill

9. It is the sheer magnitude of the number of prospects we approach that keeps us from overreacting to those who do reject our approaches.
   —Mark Yarnell

10. Just to see how serious and hungry you are, life will humble you. Pain and self-doubt will stare at you in the mirror each morning.
    —Jim Smith, Jr.

11. The best project you'll ever work on is YOU.
    —Eric Worre

12. You have to set precise goals and continuously revise those goals. —Brian Tracy

13. Just say what you mean and mean what you say. It's simple. If you say you're going to do something, DO IT. —Jim Smith, Jr.

14. Work hard in silence; let success be your noise. —Frank Ocean

15. The successful man will profit from his mistakes and try again in a different way. —Dale Carnegie

16. Network Marketing is a business of distributors building their own front lines and teaching their people how to duplicate that process. —Rene Reid Yarnell

17. It's OK if it's not for them, but it's unforgiveable if you say it's not for me! If you love me, encourage me and support me. —Larry Raskin

18. Every time you find yourself irritated or angry with someone, the one to look at is not that person but yourself. —Anthony de Mello

19. To me, awesome has no laurels to rest upon. It is an ongoing state, achieved by continuously seeking out new challenges... living each day with a purpose!
—Dan Kropp

20. Complexity is your enemy. Any fool can make something complicated. It's hard to keep things simple.
—Richard Branson

21. In Network Marketing, you will think the reward is money, but the freedom will far outweigh the money and in the end it will be all about the lives you change.
—Paula Pritchard

22. If someone offers you an amazing opportunity and you're not sure you can do it, say yes... then learn how to do it later.
—Richard Branson

23. People with a fixed mindset are too worried about the negative perception if they fail, so they end up not even trying. People with a growth mindset view challenges and setbacks as events to learn from. –Carol Dweck

24. Failure is more often a matter of "won't" rather than "can't". It's easy to have the idea of being successful, but it's not easy to make the commitment. –Brian Tracy

25. It's easier to give birth than to raise the dead. –Unknown

26. What do most of us do when we have a failure? We analyze it and languish over it and let ourselves get buried by it, when what we should do when something doesn't go our way is to simply say "next", and move on. —Richard Fenton & Andrea Waltz

27. The *Law of Attraction* says that you'll become the average of the five people you spend the most time with. You'll think how they think, act how they act, talk how they talk, and earn how they earn. —Jim Rohn

28. There is a direct correlation between the books you read and the money you make.
    —Willie Jolley

29. You become the person you think, dream and write about. —Jim Smith, Jr.

30. My best advice is: "Don't waste a minute".
    —Barbara Corcoran

31. Remember that people don't care how much you know until they know how much you care. —Jim Smith, Jr.

32. The greatest wealth is health. —Virgil

33. Fear is a tranquillizer, a sedative; it prevents action and holds us back from living a full life.
—Matthew Michalewicz

34. Rejection by friends and family is by far one of the biggest challenges in Network Marketing. But you can only change their attitude by changing your own. —Mark Yarnell

35. Motivation runs out after a few hours or a few days. You need to keep going back to the well with spaced repetition.
—Capt. Charlie Plumb

36. Rise above emotion, we can't let the emotion rule us.
    —Tony Cupisz

37. This is net-*WORK* marketing, not net-*I'll think about it* marketing, or net-*One day I'll get to it* marketing. —Holton Buggs

38. Opportunity is missed by most people because it is dressed in overalls, and looks like work.
    —Thomas Edison

39. Either you're pursuing greatness or you're just waiting to die... you better decide which one it's going to be for you. —Aaron Burt

40. Persistence, coupled with absolute belief, can never be defeated. —Mark Yarnell

41. Try to avoid reinventing the wheel when you get into this profession. —Eric Worre

42. The quality of your work will have a great deal to do with the quality of your life. —Louis Zamperini

43. Are you willing to live your life at a lower level to make other people happy? —Nekoda Bragg

44. Only take advice from people who are currently building a business. —Don Failla

45. When picking up the phone, do not fear rejection, but rather think, *"Every call I make brings me closer to a bigger business."*
   —Matthew Michalewicz

46. The foundation stones for a balanced success are honesty, character, integrity, faith, love, and loyalty. —Zig Ziglar

47. Let go of yesterday. Let today be a new beginning and be the best that you can. —Joel Osteen

48. The opposite of networking is NOT working.
   —Someone Smart

49. I've limited my associations with negative people or people who weren't helping me grow in the direction of my dreams. —Eric Worre

50. Vision keeps you hungry until you reach your goal. —James Adlam

51. Become the kind of leader that people would follow voluntarily; even if you had no title or position. —Brian Tracy

52. Whatever is it, you never finish one exposure without setting up the next one. Never! If you do, it's over. —Eric Worre

53. Almost every successful person begins with two beliefs: that the future can be better than the present, and I have the power to make it happen. —Unknown

54. During conversations, make the person you're talking to feel like he/she is the most important person in your life at that moment.
—Jim Smith, Jr.

55. You might be smarter than me, your family might come from privilege, your dad might own a company, but you WILL NOT outwork me!
—Eric Thomas

56. Most people do Network Marketing every day, but just don't get paid for it.
    —Unknown

57. Formal education will make you a living, but self-education will make you a fortune. —Jim Rohn

58. It will take about three years of consistent part-time effort in order to go full-time. It will take about five years of consistent effort to become a six-figure earner or above. And it will take about seven years of consistent effort to become an expert.
    —Eric Worre

59. Dress for success. Image is very important. People judge you by the way you look on the outside.
—Brian Tracy

60. When you're busy making money, you have no time for negative people... people who are negative are either lonely, broke or bored.
—Unknown

61. Do something every day that scares you.
—Robin Sharma

62. Change is good when your attitude is great.
—Willie Jolley

63. If you end up 40 or 50 years old and broke, it's because you value other people's opinions more than financial freedom. You became a slave to other people's opinions.
—Clif Braun

64. One of the best decisions in my life was making a career out of Network Marketing, instead of just messing around. Becoming a professional made all the difference. —Eric Worre

65. Complacency kills; floating along in the current is a choice. —Andy Andrews

66. You will be attacked when you step out of the pack. People will try to kill your dreams. –Darren Hardy

67. If you can't make it in Network Marketing where people are willing to teach you, help you, root for you, and make money with you...where can you make it? –Jeremy Bhimji

68. Suffer the pain of discipline or suffer the pain of regret. –Tony Cupisz

69. A lion never loses sleep over the opinions of sheep. –Unknown

70. Always lead with a firm handshake, eye contact and a big smile. —Denis Waitley

71. You may think the grass is greener on the other side, but if you take the time to water your own grass, it would be just as green. —Unknown

72. If you want more money in your business, stop waiting on other people. Start serving more people. Start sharing your story. Start loving your work. Start giving and you'll start receiving. —Howard Britt

73. Without desire, success is impossible. There is no commitment, nothing to push you, pull you, when you have nothing left to push and pull with.
—Matthew Michalewicz

74. If you need permission from your significant other to build something substantial for your family, then you are in the wrong relationship. —Aaron Burt

75. Bring some passion. Enthusiasm is contagious. It's okay to get a little bit fired up. —Eric Worre

76. Be the student. Find a teacher and make it happen.
—Willie Jolley

77. If my downline did what I did today, how much money would I be making?
—Brian Carruthers

78. Never judge a book by its cover, but don't hesitate to flip it over to read the summary —Chris Bostic

79. Become focused! Become consistent! Become irrational! Become purposeful! Stop trying! Say what you mean and mean what you say.
—Jim Smith, Jr.

80. You will meet people who believe all Network Marketing opportunities are pyramid schemes. Why spend all of your time trying to convince them otherwise when there are legions of people who are open to what you have?
—Randy Gage

81. Every single person you know will join your business, the only question is... are you going to quit before they do? —Unknown

82. I loved my friends, I just didn't love them enough to stay broke with them.
—James Adlam

83. The road to success has one lane but many parking spaces along the way. You alone can decide to either drive forward or park when the journey becomes difficult. —Olimpia Mihai

84. Only action can turn your goals into reality.
—Matthew Michalewicz

85. Think about how much further along your business could be if you didn't get offended... when someone won't be your customer, when they aren't interested in the business. —Danny Bae

86. You must put the whole power of your great soul into every act, however small and commonplace.
—Wallace Wattles

87. If you give up, it means you never really wanted it.
—Patrick Maser

88. Let no one discourage your ambitious attitude. You don't need a fan club to achieve your goals. Be your own motivation.
—Mama Zara

89. It takes an average of four to six exposures for the average person to join.
—Eric Worre

90. The worst thing we can do is get a second job. The BEST thing we can do is start a home-based business.
 —Dave Ramsey

91. Don't follow the crowd, let the crowd follow you!
 —Unknown

92. Observe the masses, and do the opposite. —Holton Buggs

93. If Network Marketing is so terrible, why then do thousands join every day?
 —Unknown

94. Don't let average people make you feel guilty for pursuing your life's mission.
 —Eric Worre

95. The "*Yes's*" build your business, and the "*No's*" build you. —LaToya Haynes

96. If it is important to you, you will find a way. If not, you will find an excuse.
—Unknown

97. My group grew from a few dozen to a few hundred and then to a few thousand. All I did was learn how to successfully invite people to watch a video, follow it up with an invitation to an event, and teach everyone else to do the same thing.
—Eric Worre

98. I stopped explaining myself once I realized that people only understand from their level of perception.
—Unknown

99. Every choice you make has an end result. —Zig Ziglar

100. Don't be predictable. Don't be boring. Don't ever make a dull presentation. Always think outside the box and be a differentiator.
—Harvey Mackay

101. You will never leave where you are, until you decide where you want to be.
—Dexter Yager

102. Do you want to know the real reason why people don't like Network Marketing? They run into far too many amateurs.
—Larry Raskin

103. You can make more friends in two months by becoming interested in other people than you can in two years by trying to get other people interested in you.
—Dale Carnegie

104. Don't ever let anyone steal your dreams!
—Dexter Yager

105. Fears can be learned and unlearned. You learn how to fear by creating an association between the thing you fear and some negative outcome. You can unlearn the fear if you change the association.
—Matthew Michalewicz

106. A lie... to yourself... to others... produces absolutely ZERO... it's devastating.
—Andy Andrews

107. Take care of the relationship, and the money will take care of itself. —Robin Sharma

108. We are our own worst enemy when we overcomplicate things.
—Tony Cupisz

109. Replace "can't" with "don't want to". "Can't" is a deadly venom you must extract from your life. "Can't" is for the lazy, the weak, those who like to be victims and make excuses.
—Matthew Michalewicz

110. Sort through as many people as possible to find people that are self-motivated and looking for success.
—Simon Abboud

111. Be yourself. So many people become a different person when they start inviting. This makes everyone uncomfortable. Be yourself. Just focus on being your best self.
—Eric Worre

112. Own the space you occupy... when you make the decision to be "in", you need to be "all-in".
—Larry Raskin

113. As a general rule, it will take you about one year to become competent in Network Marketing.
—Eric Worre

114. Most people have no earthly idea what they can do because all they have ever been told is what they cannot do. —Unknown

115. Having an Eastern mindset of gratitude and thankfulness will move you through the compensation plan faster than anything else. —James Adlam

116. The life meter is always ticking. Life is gone way too soon. Why is it difficult to have a forgiving spirit? —Jim Smith, Jr.

117. Where is it written that rejection has to be awful? Why can't rejection be only slightly annoying or amusing or for that matter, exciting and energizing? While we have absolutely no control over the actions of others, we do have total and complete control over how we react. —Richard Fenton & Andrea Waltz

118. A year from now, you will wish you started today. —Karen Lamb

119. Only two things will change you: inspiration or desperation. —Unknown

120. It is a race to help a person get results quickly. If they received early positive reinforcement, they'd continue. And if they didn't, they had a tendency to fade away. —Eric Worre

121. I am not worried about what broke people think of me. —Al Thomas

122. I've disassociated with the people who were toxic to my life. This isn't an easy decision, but it's an important one. Some people will keep you down permanently. —Eric Worre

123. Numbing yourself to "no" isn't about ignoring it; it's about experiencing it so often that it eventually loses its power over you. Do the thing you fear... and the fear will go away. —Richard Fenton & Andrea Waltz

124. Network Marketing gives people the opportunity, with very low risk and very low financial commitment, to build their own income-generating asset and acquire great wealth. —Robert Kiyosaki

125. We act as consultants offering suggestions on how people can live a better life. If you focus on getting a customer or new distributor, you'll constantly be disappointed and you'll find your prospects running away from you. —Eric Worre

126. You can have it all. You just can't have it all at once. —Oprah

127. The quality of your life will be determined by your ability to effectively communicate. —Unknown

128. You don't have to get it perfect, you just need to get it started.
—Joe Schoeder

129. Who is going to be committed and who is going to step up and say "This is mine, I'm going to take it!"? —Spencer Hunn

130. People lose their way when they lose their why. Know your why. —Unknown

131. Mentally and outwardly act like a president, no matter where you are in the organization.
—Tony Cupisz

132. Find out what 95% of the people in the world do, and DON'T do it... otherwise you will have what they have, and it's not much. —Al Thomas

133. I will not let anyone walk through my mind with their dirty feet.
—Mahatma Gandhi

134. Baby-sitting a downline is not an effective way to build a business.
—Mark Yarnell

135. There is no reserved sign on success.
—Barbara Corcoran

136. Professionals promote themselves as much as they promote the opportunity.
—Eric Worre

137. Discover the best path. How did others achieve what you want to achieve? Find out! All of the knowledge you need is available, waiting. Choose a path that best fits your particular circumstances.
—Matthew Michalewicz

138. Persistency, consistency, discipline, urgency, and excitement were the foundation of my success.
—Deborah Dawui

139. There is no such thing as a big problem, just a small vision. —Unknown

140. No matter how long and treacherous your journey may seem, remember... there is a light at the end of the tunnel. —Unknown

141. My willingness to hear "no" got me on the right track in my career, but it was my *wantingness* to fail that catapulted me to the top. —Richard Fenton & Andrea Waltz

142. You must emotionally detach yourself from the outcome. —Eric Worre

143. Your lack of credibility is only temporary. Longevity builds credibility.
—Unknown

144. You can make money by accident, but you won't get wealthy by accident.
—Grant Cardone

145. You need to be hungry, passionate, consistent and focused.
—Greg Provenzano

146. Success isn't for the chosen few, but for the few who choose to do great things.
—Max Knowles

147. Stop looking for your mentor to uplift you; build it yourself! Plug in and win! –Debbie Davis

148. Great works are performed not by strength but by perseverance. –Samuel Johnson

149. Don't find customers for your products, find products for your customers. –Seth Godin

150. When we are in a negative mindset, we are in the bottom half of our potential band. –Shawn Anchor

151. A wealthy person is simply someone who has learned how to make money when they're not working.
—Robert Kiyosaki

152. Read every day for one hour... something positive or containing knowledge related to your field.
—Brian Tracy

153. Everything you learn in the shallows equips you for the deep. —Unknown

154. Never say you cannot afford something. That is a poor man's attitude. Ask how to afford it.
—Robert Kiyosaki

155. Only 10% of happiness is related to the external world that we live in. 90% is how we process the world around us.
—Shawn Anchor

156. If there is something in your life you don't like, change it. If you can't change it, change your attitude. —Willie Jolley

157. Courage is not the absence of fear. Courage is acting in the face of fear. It's being afraid of something and doing it anyway.
—Richard Fenton & Andrea Waltz

158. There are a thousand excuses for failure but never a good reason. —Mark Twain

159. Failure isn't permanent. Use failure as a way to learn. —Jeremy Bhimji

160. I wish I could buy people for what they think they are worth, and sell them for what they are really worth. I would make a fortune. —Unknown

161. Your friends and family don't take you seriously because you don't take your organization seriously. —James Adlam

162. Life is such a great gift. Every choice we make either adds to or detracts from this. —Denis Waitley

163. If I had to do it all over again, rather than build an old-style type of business, I would have started building a Network Marketing business. —Robert Kiyosaki

164. If you want quantum change, it should never feel right. —Larry Raskin

165. Don't wish for less problems, wish for more skills. —Jim Rohn

166. Professionals are emotionally detached from the outcome. In other words, their goal is education and understanding while helping a prospect make a decision that would positively impact their life. —Eric Worre

167. Don't wait, the time will never be *just right*. —Napoleon Hill

168. Launching new reps: you need to get it down emotionally; we are in an emotion management business. —Larry Raskin

169. In Network Marketing, duplication is what success looks like! —Michael Clouse

170. Enthusiasm and passion are 100% required in everything you do.
—Harvey Mackay

171. The main reason most people struggle professionally and personally is simply due to a lack of focus caused by procrastination, distractions and interruptions.
—Brian Tracy

172. Nothing worth having comes easy! —Unknown

173. In the absence of value, price is always an issue.
—Tony Cupisz

174. I'm often asked if Network Marketing is a pyramid scheme. My reply is that corporations really are pyramid schemes. A corporation has only one person at the top, generally the CEO, and everyone else below.
—Donald Trump

175. The goal isn't more money. The goal is living life on your terms.
—Chris Brogan

176. Confidence is key; you can't question the opportunity.
    –Max Knowles

177. The only difference between a rich person and a poor person is how they use their time.
    –Robert Kiyosaki

178. If your business is not on the internet, then your business will be out of business. –Bill Gates

179. The richest people in the world look for and build networks, everyone else looks for work.
    –Robert Kiyosaki

180. Study and underline self-help books all of the time. –Harvey Mackay

181. Whatever you hold in your mind on a consistent basis is exactly what you will experience in your life. –Tony Robbins

182. A pessimist sees the difficulty in every opportunity, an optimist sees the opportunity in every difficulty. –Winston Churchill

183. Complaining is a zero return investment. –Gary Vaynerchuk

184. Begin with your end game in mind. Have a plan for how you will invest your earnings as they arrive.
—Brian Carruthers

185. When you learn to take ownership, you are a different breed of professional. —Tony Cupisz

186. You only win when you help others win.
—Unknown

187. Professionals are always prepared. Always. They have everything they need to get a person started right on the spot.
—Eric Worre

188. Instill daily discipline in your life; discipline has its rewards. —Larry Raskin

189. Success in this industry is not in finding the right person, but in becoming the right person.
—Dr. Forrest Shaklee

190. Ultimately, what makes it all good and keeps me positive is all about perspective. I have the power to redefine any barrier or situation based on how I choose to perceive it and receive it.
—Kimberly Cortijo

191. During conversations, focus on the other person. Learn what makes them tick. Ask, listen, observe.
—Chris Brogan

192. You have the ability to completely control your thinking, the ability to control who you are around, the ability to choose what you read/watch... more importantly, you have the ability to choose who you are *not* around, to choose what you do *not* read/watch.
—Andy Andrews

193. Wealthy people decide quickly and rarely change their minds. —Willie Jolley

194. Find out what you love to do, then dedicate yourself night and day to getting better at it. —Brian Tracy

195. Remember it's a long-term game. You will win or lose individual hands or sessions, but it's what happens in the long-term that matters. —Tony Hsieh

196. Become an avid, constant student to new information. —Brian Tracy

197. The word "no" doesn't have to be debilitating to us. That's the most important lesson you'll ever learn. —Richard Fenton & Andrea Waltz

198. In Network Marketing, you persevere or you perish. Quitting is the one sure way to fail.
—Mark Yarnell

199. I knew that goodness, intelligence, and integrity were not products of your salary but of your character.
—Jim Smith, Jr.

200. Network Marketing is living life on your own terms. No questions asked!
—Deborah Dawui

201. Nothing can compete with the word of mouth; traditional advertising does not stand a chance.
—Andy Andrews

202. One of the most common causes of failure is the habit of quitting when one is overtaken by temporary defeat. —Napoleon Hill

203. You literally have no excuse to NOT succeed; we are comfortably broke in America. —Al Thomas

204. It's always been about working hard to create an opportunity that can truly change people's lives, and we are accomplishing that goal one success story at a time. —Greg Provenzano

205. Don't think about your daily tasks that will drive your success, don't analyze them — just do them! —Matthew Michalewicz

206. There are essentially two things that will make you wise: the books you read and the people you meet. —Jack Canfield

207. Sometimes we have too much knowledge; it's not just about knowing more. You need to be able to effectively explain what you do in a simple manner.
—Craig Wortmann

208. Stop procrastinating, looking for excuses, feeling that the world isn't helping you enough. Take ownership of your goals and actions... the only time you'll ever have is now. Your half second is ticking!
—Matthew Michalewicz

209. Professionals expect the person to join because their belief that the opportunity would benefit the prospect is so strong. They are rock solid.
—Eric Worre

210. Effective communication is 20% about what you know and 80% how you feel about what you know.
—Jim Rohn

211. You need to be humble. If you are too big to serve, you are too small to lead.
—Greg Provenzano

212. Learn to understand people and human nature. Never project doubt, fear, or second guessing.
—Tony Cupisz

213. If you finish each exposure by setting up the next one, the prospect will eventually become educated on the opportunity and make an informed decision.
—Eric Worre

214. People are negative about something when they are uneducated or something bad happened in the past, this is 100% natural.
—Tony Cupisz

215. When something is important enough, you do it even if the odds are not in your favor. —Elon Musk

216. You only have control over 3 things in your life: the thoughts you think, the images you visualize, and the actions you take.
—Jack Canfield

217. Of all the entrepreneurial opportunities available today, one of the most important is direct selling, also called Network Marketing.
—Paul Zane Pilzer

218. If you are a person with big dreams and would love to support others in achieving their big dreams, then the Network Marketing business is definitely a business for you. You can start your business part-time at first and then as your business grows, you can help other people start their part-time business. This is a value worth having — a business and people who help others make their dreams come true.
—Robert T. Kiyosaki

219. The greatest source of happiness is the ability to be grateful at all times.
—Zig Ziglar

220. Network Marketing is an equal opportunity opportunity.
—Michael Clouse

221. Work with the people that DESERVE your time, not the people who want it.
—Jim Rohn

222. The poor, the unsuccessful, the unhappy, the unhealthy are the ones who use the word "tomorrow" the most.
—Robert Kiyosaki

223. Always stay humble and hungry... this is your freedom ticket! —Unknown

224. My goal is to create a life I don't need vacation from. —Rob Hill Sr.

225. Remember, our goal is education and understanding. It's not to win an argument. —Eric Worre

226. When you first meet someone, use his or her name a few times to create a feeling of familiarity. —CIO Online

227. Being hungreee requires a phenomenal amount of discipline, drive, determination, self-esteem and confidence.
—Jim Smith, Jr.

228. When you are successful, you don't ask what's wrong with something, you ask what's right with it.
—Eric Thomas

229. Wishing does not amount to anything unless it is backed by endeavor, determination and grit.
—Louis Zamperini

230. Every day in your Network Marketing business is about building. Either you are building your business, or your business is building you. —Unknown

231. You need to have a sharp, vivid picture of your goals and the kind of life you want to design for yourself.
—Matthew Michalewicz

232. When you want to succeed as bad as you want to breathe, then you will be successful. —Eric Thomas

233. How much did they pay you to give up on your dreams? —George Clooney

234. Success occurs when your dreams get bigger than your excuses. —Unknown

235. The biggest obstacles in our lives are the barriers we create in our minds. —Unknown

236. Life is a roller coaster...enjoy the ride! —Arturo Nesci

237. Nothing is more powerful than the combination of hard work toward meaningful goals. —Thomas V. Morris

238. Hearing *"yes"* is the easy part of the job and teaches you virtually nothing. But learning to hear *"no"* over and over again and to never quit... now that builds character and self-esteem. That's empowering! –Richard Fenton & Andrea Waltz

239. Professionals ask question after question after question and are great listeners. –Eric Worre

240. If people like you, they'll listen to you. But if they trust you, they'll do business with you. –Zig Ziglar

241. Understand that networking is an ongoing process, not a discrete event. Success comes from consistently making new contacts, following-up and keeping in touch.
—Smart Networking

242. People follow people with character and vision.
—Tony Cupisz

243. When you start with urgency and a compliment, it becomes very difficult for a person to react negatively to your invitation. —Eric Worre

244. The key to living like a king is to work like a slave.
—Unknown

245. You can work with 100, but you can't carry three on your back. —Jim Rohn

246. Self-belief is critical to success. Studies have shown that belief about your capabilities is a more accurate predictor of success than your actual capabilities.
—Matthew Michalewicz

247. Don't mistake movement for achievement. Eliminate wasted time.
—Jim Rohn

248. If there's no mess, then there's no message. That's why I know anyone can be awesome. But you have to be open to pain and possibilities, and push back and be persistent. When in trouble, I go back to my roots, my lessons, my beliefs, and my Titans. —Jim Smith, Jr.

249. There is no elevator to success... you have to take the stairs. —Eric Worre

250. You need to be a value creator in your industry. —Larry Raskin

251. It is easy to believe in your company, but you have to believe in yourself to be successful. —Max Knowles

252. The quality of your life will be determined in direct proportion by how effectively you communicate.
—Tony Cupisz

253. When everyone else says it's impossible and you'll fail, your personal commitment to your dream provides another voice that says you will persevere and win.
—Unknown

254. It's very important that people develop an emotional attachment to the products and that can only happen if they are using them and enjoying the benefits. —Eric Worre

255. To earn more, you must learn more. —Brian Tracy

256. Those who offend the least, make the most.
—Casey Snyder

257. You need to have a radical assault on your status quo. Put your head down, work extremely hard, and don't come up for air!
—Greg Provenzano

258. You can either make money or you can make excuses, but you can't do both! —Debbie Davis

259. Champions live different than normal people. —Willie Jolley

260. Being lazy, having a sense of entitlement, and coasting is the worst thing that can happen to you. —Brian Tracy

261. Start small and dream big! —Robert Kiyosaki

262. I already know what giving up feels like. I want to see what happens if I don't. —Unknown

263. Power of influence goes beyond people; what you put in your mind has the same effect. Everything you read, see and hear influences you. You need to become conscious of what you put into your head... you are in control!
   —Matthew Michalewicz

264. If nothing changes, nothing changes. If one thing changes, everything changes!
   —Mathieu Ambroise

265. I'm doing this with or without you, but I would rather it be with you.
   —Unknown

266. A friendship founded on business is better than a business founded on friendship.
—John D. Rockefeller, Jr

267. Most people have been programmed to be worker bees; you need to develop an entrepreneurial mindset. —Al Thomas

268. 100% of the people in your car will show up!
—Unknown

269. Action creates motivation. If you are waiting for motivation to come to you, do something!
—Tony Cupisz

270. Self-belief flows from our environment. Our beliefs, attitudes and values are largely the product of our environmental forces. This influence doesn't stop at childhood, it continues throughout life until the very end. The implications are enormous.
—Matthew Michalewicz

271. As soon as you seek to inspire others, it inspires the best in you.
—Brendon Burchard

272. Network Marketing is the greatest opportunity in the history of capitalism.
—Mark Yarnell

273. If you rest too long, the weeds take over the garden in the summer. Life doesn't stand still, and random negativity will start overwhelming the positive arrangements of life if you just let things go. —Jim Rohn

274. Whatever you are thinking, think bigger. —Unknown

275. Dream big and dare to fail. —Norman Vaughn

276. Be quick to let stuff go; there are always better things to come in life. —Willie Jolley

277. Home based businesses are one of the fastest growing segments in our economy and that trend will only continue as the age of the corporation, which began barely a century ago, now gives way to the age of the entrepreneur.
—Paul Zane Pilzer

278. Do the uncomfortable until it becomes comfortable.
—Unknown

279. Constantly feed your mind with the images, words, thoughts, information and aspirations you desire.
—Jim Smith, Jr.

280. Right now someone far less qualified than you is living your dreams. All because they didn't just think about it, they took action!
—Brad Sugars

281. Visualization is a powerful weapon against fear. If you watch a scary movie 10 or 20 times, the movie isn't scary anymore because you know what happens next, you've seen it before. By visualizing something a number of times in your mind, your fear is reduced when it comes to the real thing.
—Matthew Michalewicz

282. You have to be excited and truly believe in your organization for it to work. —Max Knowles

283. Don't just work harder than the next guy, work harder than everybody else. —Vince Lombardi

284. Always be prospecting wherever you go: how you show up, being an attractive walking billboard, lifting people up, being interested in others (saying less), discovering people. You need to plant seeds for the long-term. —Larry Raskin

285. Your regrets of inaction will last longer and cut deeper than other regrets because psychologically they're more "open" and boundless; you'll never know what *might have been*. If you try and fail, your regret will be short-lived. But if you never try, your regret will be life-long.
—Matthew Michalewicz

286. If you don't want to listen, don't want to read and don't want to learn... you aren't getting anywhere good in life.
—Grant Cardone

287. To conquer fear, your desire must be rioting in your heart; that kind of desire will strangle fear.
—Matthew Michalewicz

288. Let me give you my formula for financial independence in Network Marketing: Your ability to get a large group of people to consistently do a few simple things over an extended period of time.
—Eric Worre

289. You need to enroll full-time to succeed; practice, drill, rehearse, play, rewind.
—Larry Raskin

290. Network Marketing is the big wave of the future. It's taking the place of franchising, which now requires too much capital for the average person. —Jim Rohn

291. If you want great success in Network Marketing, you must become masterful with your language. Use your words to paint the picture of where they can be in 3-5 years down the road. —Larry Raskin

292. The more you give, the more you get. —Unknown

293. Any kind of a human being can wish for a thing, can desire it. But only strong, vigorous minds with a great purpose can do things. There is an infinite distance between the wishers and the doers. –Louis Zamperini

294. Freely give your time, resources and support to people who could benefit from your talents, wisdom and skills. –Jim Smith, Jr.

295. Take ownership of your own business; none of the top earners looked for a handout. –Al Thomas

296. Quit making excuses, putting it off, complaining about it, believing you can't, worrying if you can, waiting until you are older, skinnier, richer, braver, or all around better. Suck it up, hold on tight, make a plan and just do it! –Unknown

297. People don't buy what you do… they buy why you do it. –Simon Sinek

298. You can't have a million dollar dream with a minimum wage work ethic. –Zig Ziglar

299. The best follow-up question I've ever used is, "What did you like best?"
—Eric Worre

300. It's more important to grow your income than cut your expenses. It is more important to grow your spirit than cut your dreams. —Robert Kiyosaki

301. If you rely on circumstance, your business depends on luck. If you rely on skill, you can make it happen whenever you want. Focus on skill!
—Tony Cupisz

302. Every day needs to be a working day. —Al Thomas

303. If someone uses the word "pyramid" with me, I always say, "Oh no. Pyramid schemes are illegal, and I would never be involved with something illegal. —Eric Worre

304. When you change your thinking, you change your future.
—Mark Victor Hansen

305. Momentum is created by brand new and excited reps following the system.
—Max Knowles

306. People respect a person who does what they say they're going to do. People also respect a person who values their own time.
—Eric Worre

307. First, you have to be visible in the community. You have to get out there and connect with people. It's not called net-sitting or net-eating. It's called networking. You have to work at it.
—Dr. Ivan Misner

308. Rich people don't work for their money, their money works for them.
—Al Thomas

309. Don't make the mistake that results in nearly 50% of failures in our industry: building your front line for the first few months, then stopping to manage your people. —Mark Yarnell

310. Excuses are the nails used to build the house of failure. —Greg Sarlo Jr.

311. Do not underestimate discipline. If you need to make 5 calls and only make 1, you are down 4 calls. Harm has been done here! Compound this over a full year and it adds up big time. —Jim Rohn

312. Be in a hurry to live. Live each day like it's a dream. Live each year like it's your last. Enjoy life down to the last drop, the last taste, the very last millisecond. Because dream or not, you only have half a second — so make the most of your days left, do everything you want to, and do it now, before it's too late... before you wake up...
—Matthew Michalewicz

313. Believe in yourself and always have integrity and focus. —LuAn Mitchell

314. If something isn't popular, you are likely on the right track. —Larry Raskin

315. Never, never treat time as if you had an unlimited supply. —Og Mandino

316. If you become teachable and remain so, a Network Marketing career will make you money. More importantly it will mold your character.
—Jay Vandenhoff

317. Leaders don't look for recognition from others, leaders look for others to recognize. —Simon Sinek

318. Time is more valuable than money. You can always get more money, but you cannot get more time.
—Jim Rohn

319. Remembering that you are going to die is the best way that I know to avoid the trap of thinking you have something to lose.
—Steve Jobs

320. Whatever you don't master will have mastery over you.
—Max Knowles

321. Fear = Progress. It is impossible to achieve success without fear.
—Matthew Michalewicz

322. Everything is a big deal unless you have the vision.
 —James Adlam

323. People buy from other people due to likeability and chemistry. You need to display a keen interest in others.
 —Harvey Mackay

324. Be careful who you pretend to be, you might forget who you really are.
 —Bob Marley

325. If you act like a champion, you will become a champion.
 —George St. Pierre

326. The Network Marketing profession does over $182 billion dollars a year in retail sales. Maybe it's time you take a closer look.
—Eric Worre

327. Being prepared is different than being ready.
—Larry Raskin

328. You need to put your head down and get to work. Someone is going to be successful in Network Marketing, why not make it you? —Al Thomas

329. Recruit the best, they recruit the rest.
—Unknown

330. Commitment is doing what you need to do even when you don't want to.
—Jim Smith, Jr.

331. Human behavior is identical to the animal kingdom. The weak (complainers/excuses) will be knocked out (eaten by lions), making room for new growth. —Al Thomas

332. Success comes to people with leadership skills, a sound vision, enthusiasm, and the willingness to put forth the effort to build an organization and find others who will do the same. —Rene Reid Yarnell

333. For building a large and duplicating organization, I have found that a tool is a better first step. Remember, our goal is education and understanding. We want people to know what we have and understand how it can benefit their lives.
—Eric Worre

334. Do not brag or boast of yourself; simply live in a great way.
—Wallace Wattles

335. What people *can* do is very different from what they *will* do. —Tony Robbins

336. We are in the midst of a boom in home-based businesses, and it shows no signs of slowing.
—Paul Zane Pilzer

337. Be committed to the process without being emotionally attached to the results. —Hal Elrod

338. Since we've been conditioned and socialized to work until we're exhausted and to always wait for significant occasions to plan something special, we settle into a BORING, daily routine. —Jim Smith, Jr.

339. Never wish it were easier, wish that you were better.
—Jim Rohn

340. Say goodbye forever to the excuses. You have to get out of your own way and hold yourself responsible for your tomorrows.
—Jim Smith, Jr.

341. Apply the question "why" to your greatest successes.
—Andy Andrews

342. Are you doing what you love? Or just what is expected of you?
—Anthony Peters

343. Vision without action is a daydream. Action without vision is a nightmare.
—Japanese Proverb

344. The only person you are destined to become is the person you decide to be.
—Ralph Waldo Emerson

345. If you do what you've always done, you'll get what you've always gotten.
—Tony Robbins

346. You will never change your life until you change something you do daily. The secret of your success is found in your daily routine. —John Maxwell

347. There's something magical about audio. It whispers in your ear, reminding you of your dreams, of your potential and how to get there. In addition, it's repetitive. —Eric Worre

348. The question we should be asking: *Would I want to be sponsored by me?*
—Jeff Olson

349. Winners work. They sweat, sacrifice and take action. They avoid becoming complacent when things are going well. Remember, complacency kills.
—Robin Sharma

350. I cannot be awesome if I'm always worrying about what other people think. Besides, some people are just not going to clap anyway. But that's OK. —Jim Smith, Jr.

351. I realized that failure was the halfway mark on the road to success, not a destination to be avoided but rather a stepping stone to get what I really wanted in life. —Richard Fenton & Andrea Waltz

352. I can teach you everything I know about this business, but I can't give you desire. —Ben Mihai

353. The very best people deliberately practice to get the best results possible in their position at the time.
—Brian Tracy

354. If you understand the human element of Network Marketing, you can win long-term.
—Greg Provenzano

355. Expect the best... in the long run you will probably get it. —Denis Waitley

356. You cannot consistently perform in a manner that is inconsistent with what you believe.
—Jim Smith, Jr.

357. The future of Network Marketing is unlimited. There's no end in sight. It will continue to grow, because better people are getting into it. They are raising the entire standard of MLM to the point where soon, it will be one of the most respected business methods in the world.
—Brian Tracy

358. People feed off of your confidence.
—Jim Smith, Jr.

359. Success has ruined many a man. —Ben Franklin

360. Part of the reason people avoid taking action is they are afraid they'll be embarrassed. If you want to be successful in Network Marketing, you must learn to set that fear aside.
—Eric Worre

361. Most of you won't be successful... not because you can't do it, but because you can't outlast your *old* you long enough to get to your *new* you.
—Eric Thomas

362. If you really want something, you have to go after it hard until you get it. —Tony Cupisz

363. If you are doing what everyone else is doing and thinking what everyone else is thinking... you are probably doing something wrong. You are nothing more than average.
—Andy Andrews

364. New distributors crave direction and they respond incredibly well to simple assignments. —Eric Worre

365. The best advertising you can have is a loyal customer spreading the word about how incredible your business is.
—Shep Hyken

366. I never dreamed about success, I worked for it.
—Estee Lauder

367. Change your belief into certainty; that will take you over the top.
—Unknown

368. Holding onto anger is like drinking poison and expecting the other person to die. —Buddha

369. Losers are people who are afraid of losing.
—Robert Kiyosaki

370. Losers quit when they fail. Winners fail until they succeed. —Zig Ziglar

Well, you have reached the end of this book. It has been very difficult trying to narrow it down to my favorite quotes of all time. I hope that these quotes helped you on days where you needed an extra boost to maximize your success.

P.S. I added in a couple of bonus quotes for you, mostly because I couldn't get all the way down to the final 365. I hope you enjoyed them! :)

This book is also available for digital download if you would like to keep it on your phone or tablet for quick reference or for a little pocket motivation.

Please visit us at www.littlebookofquotes.com

www.ingramcontent.com/pod-product-compliance
Lightning Source LLC
Chambersburg PA
CBHW021435170526
45164CB00001B/254